ANTHROPOCENE BLUES

Advance Praise

John Lane's poems sing "our rich niche secured by our own pecking," with all the gorgeous ambivalence such a phrase—at once bitterly ironic and genuinely praiseful—reveals. The central nerve of this book is the long, wandering-but-broken poem "Erosion," which shows our cultural and ecological wearing-away but also what connections are revealed in that slough, what bones are unburied, what contradictions are compressed into close proximity. *Anthropocene Blues* does the vital work of close observation, unsentimental and expansive in scope, that is always the lifeblood of poetry.

—Elizabeth Bradfield, author of *Once Removed*

For John Lane the blue notes vibrate with deep time resonating in our present dilemmas. He is fully alive to the questions they raise in their freshly seen metaphors, always embedded in the muddy waters of materiality, but inevitably, he knows, mediated by modern technology. Between fox pad and IPad, the poems here pursue a fertile inquiry.

—Terry Gifford, author *Whale Watching with a Boy and a Goat*

To give our best attention to the natural world might be said to be the duty of any thoughtful citizen of the Anthropocene. But to give it with verve, humor and compassion, to celebrate its small survivals and grieve its losses with large-hearted wisdom takes a poet with the capacious vision of John Lane. *Anthropocene Blues* is a book to be thankful for.

—Don McKay, author of *Angular Unconformity: Collected Poems*

ALSO BY JOHN LANE

POETRY COLLECTIONS
The Old Rob Poems
Abandoned Quarry: New & Selected Poems
Noble Trees (with photographers Mark Olencki & Mark Dennis)
Against Information & Other Poems
As the World Around Us Sleeps

PROSE
Coyote Settles the South
Fate Moreland's Widow (a novel)
Web of Water: Reflections of Life Along the Saluda & Reedy Rivers (with
    photographers Tom Blagdon, Clay Bolt, jon holliway, and Ben Geer Keys)
My Paddle to the Sea
The Best of the Kudzu Telegraph (essays)
Begin with Rock, End with Water (essays)
Circling Home
Chattooga: Descending into the Myth of Deliverance River
Waist Deep in Black Water (essays)
Weed Time: Essays from the Edge of a Country Yard

LIMITED EDITIONS
*The Once-Again Wilderness: Following Wendell Berry into the
    Red River Gorge* (with Jeremy L.C. Jones)
The Dead Father Poems
The Body Poems
Quarries
Thin Creek

ONE-ACT PLAY
The Pheasant Cage

EDITED
Literary Dogs & their South Carolina Writers (with Betsy Wakefield Teter)
Cornbread & Sushi: A Journey Through the Rural South (with Deno Trakas)
A Packet for Vince Miller (with Donald Griener)
Hub City Christmas (with Betsy Wakefield Teter)
Hub City Anthology (with Betsy Wakefield Teter)
The Woods Stretched for Miles: New Nature Writing from the South (with Gerald
    Thurmond)
Usumacinta River Journey: A Collaborative Journal

ANTHROPOCENE BLUES

Poems

John Lane

MERCER UNIVERSITY PRESS | *Macon, Georgia*
2017

MUP/ P549

© 2017 by Mercer University Press
Published by Mercer University Press
1501 Mercer University Drive
Macon, Georgia 31207
All rights reserved

9 8 7 6 5 4 3 2 1

Books published by Mercer University Press are printed on acid-free paper
that meets the requirements of the American National Standard for
Information Sciences—Permanence of Paper for Printed Library Materials.

ISBN   978-0-88146-625-6
Cataloging-in-Publication Data is available from the Library of Congress

CONTENTS

ACKNOWLEDGMENTS

"Voice, While it Lasts" in *Asheville Poetry Review.*

"While Snorkeling the Geologist Encounters E.O. Wilson and his Book

The Social Conquest of Earth" as "While Snorkeling at the Indians near Norman Island, I Think of E.O. Wilson's Newest Book *The Social Conquest of Earth*" in *Tar River Poetry.*

"Field Notebook: Spring" and "Field Notebook: Boat Hippies" in *Flycatcher.*

"Cirque of the Towers" and "Field Notebook: Antelope Among Cattle" in *ISLE.*

A portion of "DOR" as "Dead Porcupine, Dead Radial Tire" in *Clover.*

"Poem Without an End" in *Town Creek Poetry.*

"The Geologist Anticipates the End of Time" as "The Long Count" in *House Organ.*

"The Truth About the Present" was chosen as one of the Academy of American Poets' "Poem-a-Day" project in 2011 and can be found at Poets.org.

"The Geologist Speaks of Phosphate" appears in the anthology *Found Anew,* edited by Ray McManus and R. Mac Jones (USC Press, 2015).

ANTHROPOCENE BLUES

"…a conference on geology
The thirty-fourth of its kind
In Brisbane, Australia
Is gearing up to bestow
The age we're all embarked on
With the fine name of the Anthropocene.
Will you be glad to learn
That at the very moment that the poets
Have abandoned all hope, even,
Of giving form to the human,
It's up to the learned societies
To hug this giant to their hearts…?"

—Bruno Latour Frédérique Ait-Touati,
& Chloé Latour

"I'm so lonesome I could cry."
—Hank Williams

ANTHROPOCENE BLUES

THE GEOLIGIST ON OYSTER FACTORY ROAD

I listen for the blue notes,
an older assemblage, you know, blue crab-
old, or even lichen-old, not mammalian,
more like crickets chanting in the live oaks,
or the wind full of plaintive compositions.
And what of pluff mud, riddled with stalks
of dead cordgrass, a compendium
drafted in a single seasonal supplication?

In the chorus of caucusing herring gulls
I hear woodshedding,
but I'm the block's new kid, can't crash
the circle of song, but I try anyway—

I attend the formations of pelicans
retreating to their distant sanctuaries—
If they sing, it is only there, keeping
their own monkish counsel above
the shell-clacking bank and strand—

An old man walks the beach
with a red metal detector—
His wife next to him carries
a plastic bag of black fossils picked
from the tide's wrack line.
Like minor chords remaining from
an aria scored a million years ago,
and she's still listening—
He doesn't care, wearing big
earphones as if the sand is hip-hop—

I believe in words
but this morning that faith may be
misplaced, like looking for sharks'
teeth, how you scan the sand for a break
in the pattern and not the tooth itself.
Maybe you don't listen for the song

either—maybe listening is like the way
names remain on maps long after
the thing itself—

You see, my hobby is the least tern,
splashing offshore, each dive a dart
of song from a failing concert hall—
If I listen closely I will disappear,
like the tide receding, or the tiny
fiddler crabs secure in their shallow holes.

VOICE, WHILE IT LASTS

*"Like a bird's life, it seems to be
an alternation of flights and perchings."*
—William James

Just today, talking
with a friend about voice
I said, I mean the physical
voice, our mechanical identities
as in how words squeeze out
of our throats, what we "say,"
and then if we are poets,
(as we both say we are)
how voice is assembled

sounds when a poem
is spoken out loud, and how
our voice may be the only unique
human artifact we throw at the universe
unfolding at our fingertips daily,
what is our species alone
(some of us having given up soul,
tools, and language like
a retreating army) and so

if we lose voice we
might just relinquish that
which marks us
purely human. But voice,
I added, is not a retreat,
but a collective identity,
not a withdrawal, an advance
into territory only settled by us,
as in, "the voice of the people,"

accent, rhythm. "Class.
Place-bound. There are
boundaries to the sounds we
make. You don't see birds

3

bickering about poetry
or the vagaries of voice,
do you?" But are we not birds
calling in a flock, and voice,
our shifting borders,

as the human voice is traced
by the Henry Higgins
of the world? Like another friend
who wrote me about an encounter—
"I heard your voice today
in the voice of a black teenager
in a class I was teaching." He asked
the boy where his parents
were from. "They were from where

you were born, your voice, his voice,
place and space and sound
like birds leaving a tree together."
But strolling the boardwalk
I cast out my optimism, thinking
about proposed extinctions,
and I saw a raft of bay
scoters diving along the quay,
and as they floated I tried
calling to them, finding a shared

voice they would acknowledge,
like calling to the last car of a train
leaving to a city wracked by calamity,
but they kept their distance
a few feet off the riprap, preening,
and then I turned away and saw
the Parrot Rescue man had his birds
out, including one oddly named
Scooter, a large calm African Grey

who said "here" and offered one
long finger talon as I passed,
balancing on the other foot,

and since I'd paid my five bucks
to the cause I could hold one bird
and get a picture. Scooter
climbed on my shoulder and slipped
down onto my hand
and held lightly to my collar

and pulsed his rump and rotated
cooing lightly, "here."
"He's a masturbator," the rescue
man whispered. "That's
probably why he was abandoned."
Scooter could live half-a-hundred
years and learn a thousand words,
not just vocabulary but associating
simple human sounds with meanings,

and then apply abstract concepts
of shape, color, number, but the bird's
affection pointed to me as warmer than
the simple association of words and object.
Scooter loved my hand and I let
him, an exchange between species,
a distance breeched much greater
than the few yards out to the diving
ducks, a respite in an age

of loss as the extinction spike
climbs the Y axis. As he circled
his butt I felt atavistic and warm,
beyond even a neighborly
handshake, he was a voice crying
out in the universe
for kinship and connection.
What if these African Greys

and bay scoters on the waterfront
with their comic bullseye beaks
and practiced specific dives
are already nature's afterthought

and in a century their genetic path
closes down and offers little
more than a dry hump?

THE GEOLOGIST SUSPECTS GOD PLAYS DICE

Not the puffin chick, the black-back gull.
Not the cliff mealy and green with guano
or bald eagles gorged on herring gull chicks
but the tourists passing after whales,
the windows open, the wind shifted their way.
Not our guide saying, "We call this shit cove
and you'll soon know why," gunning the black
Zodiac after breaching humpbacks and minke pods.
Not his jokes about young puffins hanging
out in cliffside bars—
Not his story of killer whales ripping apart feeding
minkes one season, but the common murre
and their colony, 100,000 strong, after less
than a thousand, forty years ago.
And how could it not be the silt stone shore,
Doctor Cove, where rock was split and tumbled
in a game of craps eons long, Mr. Einstein—
Or not the murre's dark meat the locals
still eat in winter so tough they cook a sea
stone with it "and when the murre's done,
throw way the bird, and eat the stone."

DOR*

Road kill is mind kill—some driver
lost in diminishing human
consciousness brought on
by modernity. The dead porcupine
displays his interior colors like
a brand. Quills once made into Truro
ceremonial headdresses and beaded
pouches. Now quills dissolve to greasy
stains. If we slowed down maybe
the whole wild ecosystem would be
overrun with porcupines. We are
nature's hungriest predator. We are
clearing the shoulders for kith and kin.

*

The groundhog's last
pavement belly-surf shaped
a question: "*O renegade
kin, blimped-out biped, was that
fossil salad you just burped to drive
you to my-last-there worth the cost
to either of us, drunk on our own
warm-blooded Post-epocal brew?*"

* Dead On Road

8

FOX SPARROW

Flight vector—due north—
sealed fate and folly,
the fact of our settlement,

cruel and decisive, cold
as reflective pane, clear as a slap,
or hidden snare—

Like my friend who woke to
yellow warblers, necks
broken, stiff on the deck

same day each spring—
A foraging species
of least concern—

A flight path undercut
and carnage assured
by new home construction—

The course set, the bearings—
The fluttering dying wings—
The alternate coming and goings

of last breaths after concussion—
Seasonal disorder,
the bird-brained patterns

of movement, that is,
until stopped dead
in their tracks—or paths—

Invisible doom—
The window that opens
only for us from within—

Something old and pure
moves them north in summer,
south in winter, right

through forests they
still see reflected— killing fields,
slaughterhouses, death rows—

bird in the hand—
What's left in the bush
sweet sweet sweet—

In the sparrow woods—
and yet still they move—
no choice we say

instincts of caloric
regimes, nesting material,
predators, an inventory of need

I hold out, grieve—imagine—
Calculate— this isn't science,
this data is pure poetry.

EROSION

"We can write poems that disintegrate before the reader's eyes."
        —A.R. Ammons

The present erodes, each online search, or was there ever
a present to start with? Photos stored off-site, "in the cloud"

as we say (and let me tell you, there are enough
clouds to go around these days), no hold, or holds, barred

in the fist fight we call a digital culture, like those photos
on Facebook we wish to disappear: they're somewhere

in a million Google data servers (centers?) worldwide
using 220 megawatts of power, that's mega-fleets

of servers, sometimes as many as ten million computers
connection-to-connection, to power up for all those searches

by possible or nosy current employers (what were we thinking:
shirt off, beer pong, shit-faced?): why search unless something

is really lost, and what is, that is the question, begs all
those useless trivia answers, conundrums, cacaphonies

information feeding our brains, fogging the windshield
of what matters: like the death (like death) on the Chattooga

a rafting tourist fallen out at Jawbone, swept in high water
(all this rain) into Sock-em-Dog, the body snagged somewhere

in the real maelstrom, or the dead woman on the Potomac
swept from her kayak below Great Falls, or the other

tourist in Swimmers Rapid on the Youghiogheny
his leg caught in a discarded throw rope,

(called a "safety rope" by one report), the stories moving
 on Google, one search after another: they're all three

dead, no matter how much living remains in currents
of ones and zeros moving server-to-server, posted

on Facebook, pictures, tributes, video shot weeks before
(so funny then, so painful to watch now) of her running

a waterfall, the view count heading toward viral
now she's dead: there are ghosts we all see, just out

the corner of our eyes, fog moving in our valley
where there is no fog, but these digital ghosts don't go away,

(at least until the solar flare or the half-mile wide asteroid
predicted by a panel of experts on The Weather Channel)

web pages left up, abandoned like the Bi-Lo grocery,
the roof collapsed, the windows like eyes thumbed shut:

the messages piled up in Gmail, comments, numbers still live
(for dead people) on Skype, these will never compost,

like discarded beer koozies in a black plastic bag,
our digital life built up toward heaven in its ghost mound:

WHILE SNORKELING THE GEOLOGIST
ENCOUNTERS E.O. WILSON AND HIS BOOK
THE SOCIAL CONQUEST OF EARTH

Floating like detritus through the national park
I kick a time or two, pass the urchins and seaweed
and, damn, this aquatic tourist community waves back
as their eusocial cousin visits from the upper
world of clear air and hard-won symbolic culture—

Some say all this led to me, distant bipedal kin
now pushing the whole of life toward the Sixth Great
Extinction, and I'll admit it's this gnarly drama
that's on my mind, my pleasure island reading
E.O. Wilson's study of the whole of life from early sponges
to the production of yachts for the tourist trade winds—

Suspended in my 60,000 year old intellectual bubble
I marvel at reefs still carrying on like soldiers
in the great campaign of life, transcribed
half a billion years before we got our pleistocene draft cards—

Didn't this invertebrate district get the memo?
Above their brittle ghetto floats the planet's boss,
the big chief, the emperor of air, diesel fuel,
bow thrusters, and tax shelters. Yet down here
life goes on, though bleached of much of its color
by our modern chemical toxins. I'm trying to put it all
together in my poet's watery grasp, what Keats
famously called "negative capability," and I expel
another scenario up my snorkel: we are so many billion
bubbles in a briny blue melodrama with no choreographer
and a set eaten by termites and ants—
Should we really applaud how the show never closes?

A few more nibbling fish and I try another morality
tale: maybe my ancestor's a flippered
Cortez and the squid and parrot fish don't know
the colonial ships named *You're Screwed* and *La Doce Vita*

landed two million years ago when the big brained apes
a lot like me came down from the trees. Then I round
a drowned point and there is Dr. E.O. Wilson himself,
a big old barracuda come in from the deep water—
I watch as his fixed eyes pass over me like nothing,
a snorkeling poet, a sea cow, a moving point among
the flowing arms of briny fans feeding on zoo plankton—
Wilson cruises on, gulping once or twice, devouring
the minnows of Religion, Philosophy, and Art as he passes—

Feeding, feeding, feeding, we all go at it in our own way—
Mine lacks much of the Enlightenment rigor of Dr. Wilson's
new theoretical chapters on the history of evolution—
No barracuda, I take in my calories from Romantic experience
and build my own exoskeleton like the coral tips rubbed raw
below me. I muse on how Keats would have liked snorkeling,
and how my three trips here in twenty years have built a new
colony of ideas and images, piling up within like an artificial

reef around a sunken steamer. The torpedo fish passes again
and it's a real barracuda, not Dr. Wilson after all,
and interested this time only in my shiny wedding ring,
so I hightail it for the Beneteau, leave Wilson's imaginary
forms behind and get real about the intellectual food chain.

THE GEOLOGIST FINALLY SYNTHESIZES THE
IDEA OF ISLAND BIOGEOGRAPHY

Goats on the road are miniature
isolated temples of animal vigil,
yellow eyes fixed on my brief visit

as I pass by in my own feeding—
And then the gulls on the harbor,
diving headlong into a roiling frenzy—
The sun clears the hills but can't

contain the bay's intention
to settle into a testament of green—
Everything flowing is holy—

Everything fixed is not,
so says the mind, among
turquoise edges and a rocky spine—

What of the yachtsman
paused with his cup of coffee,
and the honey bee
far from land he strikes down
on the windy deck in mid-flight?

Later, the woman at the beach bar
tells me, as if she clearly understands
evolution's maze, "Take it easy,"
and pulls her pinched fingers
into a single long slow invisible line.

FISH WITH HEAD STILL ON

Sweet flesh from reef refuge,
tail fried crispy in lard,
careful with fork and fingers
to cleave the superstructure
of fluid movement and white
flesh, perfect formations pencil
thick, aboriginal flavors,
island fruit, fins, sharp barbs—
You take a bite of Johnnycake
but grease-fixed eyes can't
quell your old bone fear,
that fish-camp terror,
that dangerous flavor.

FIELD NOTEBOOK: SPRING

A man thinks *hammerhead*, and remembers the moment a decade earlier sailing in the Abacos when a friend snorkeling on a reef had reentered the boat as if the sea itself had shrunken to that spot of disturbance. There had been two couples sailing, the man and his lover, and the man who saw the shark and his wife, and a woman in her forties, single still. Now one couple is divorced, the man and his lover are married, and the single woman's married too, but no longer keeps her captain's certification, her husband a software executive with a beach house on the nearby shore to spread out her longing for the sea into manageable, affordable weekends.

The sea, the man thinks, is a metaphor too lovely to reduce to threat. Only the force of his circling mind holds the shark memory to this place—wide view off a peaceful porch of nothing but blue bay—and not that. A shark can live decades and they say memory burns deeper—as sound, they say—extends outward through the universe. Snorkeling is a recreation replete in memory, and couples when traveling together always stow their future resolve and never consider they'll risk it diving on some reef for the chance to see what's below. Here, this sea is so shallow that boats flounder in spots it seems that to pass is natural, ignoring unheeded warnings, lights, and a battery of testimonials from those who have sailed before. Walking the beach the man thinks his own marriage is an island standing above that shallow sea.

The high tide's in a few hours, but that rise and fall is natural as wind—which they didn't have that day they saw the shark. Now she walks in the sand and he is still in the surf, just offshore, and again he thinks *hammerhead* and wonders if the shark is still alive, or is it dead? He says *marriage* and the word feels more like a shark than the sea. The movement. The ceaseless searching of commitment. Like a vacation from the universe's own menu for chaos. Two knitted together briefly, in grief and joy, the bond beyond the clarity of seawater.

The man shapes his two hands like man and wife and holds the water as long as possible. His palms are wrinkled and white, and she says, having waded in, "You can see the bottom if you open them." He lets the water flow drain back into the larger vessel. He looks, and there below is the shore moving under him as she said it would be—shells, sand, seaweed, and under it all the hard marl that the islands are made of, what keeps them standing above the churning sea.

AFTER THE GREAT ACCELERATION

The Hotel Milan, Hangzhou

There were sheer curtains with no exit to the East
There were tables of blue marble, and the rooms had shag
the color of coral. The toothpicks had holes in the middle

There was a place called Freedom right down the block
There was a place of infinite allegories to the West
There was a place ending in exceptions known only to the locals
There was a place, but it was lost to green tea, export grade
There was a place at the feet of a thousand styrene Buddhas

THE TRUTH ABOUT THE PRESENT

When rivers are intoxicated
with dioxide you gather lotus shoots
to pick their pockets is
the clock of the age

When the last songbird
shivers with undue cold like wires overhead
to handle harsh metals is
the clock of the age

When your keyboard dissolves
in the pit of nations
to write in echoes is
the clock of the age

When you forge transparencies
in the foundries upstream
the bridges are blocked by karaoke
their digital sand is
the clock of the age

The cellphone's face is always
time-dependent on fingers somewhere
today opens to the nearby delta
and tomorrow
is the clock of the age

ROAD TRIP TO SUZHOU

I'd rather follow the ancient allegiances
of water but will simply give over
to the song unfolding
on the roadsides

In articulated absences between
raised highways and fallow fields
I'd rather see the day turn tumblers
of light and fade into sodden smog
the dustbin overturns
and out flows a flower of light
refracted in the ancient glass
of Lingering Garden

Trees here are pruned beyond anger
but maybe the new leaves alleviate
discord in the forest
a lantern is certainly posted far ahead
and it brings trucks and drivers
to a halt

Bells could be in temples
or they could simply be leftovers
from another century now
festering in a cesspool along the road
silk was once a cultural certainty
but now factories migrate
to an outer district where
the worms lose their way and leaves
curl inward like dollars

I'd rather walk a foreign road
to the port where the old empire
steams home tomorrow

FIELD NOTEBOOK: BOAT HIPPIES

Captain Mark says there aren't many left, and there used to be plenty. "Everybody's so serious about their money now, even the young. Nobody comes here to disappear." Now most everything is high-dollar charters or owner-leased yachts, like the La Sonata we've rented, anchored off Foul Cay for snorkeling.

I remember back thirty years to Cumberland Island and the harbor where the boat hippy sailed in one day and anchored off the point in his sloop. He'd built the boat in his parents' backyard outside Boston as he worked nine to five downtown. It took three years to lay the keel, build up the hull, and launch. It cost almost as much to haul the boat to the harbor as it did to sail south to Granada and back north again in five more years. I'd row out to his boat and sit and talk esoteric world religions, mostly a mystic the boat hippy followed named Alice Bailey. He'd make tea and quote from Bailey's book, a blue paperback, *Ponder on This*: "Deep inside of us all a huge potential beckons, waiting to open us to joy, genius, freedom, and love within."

THE GEOLOGIST ANTICIPATES THE END OF TIME

The Mayans named it the Long Count and described their days with snakes, frogs, water lilies, and crocodiles—all the things we've named, put in field guides, bled of terror. Wading a slough back of Akumal after a thunderstorm I think of Black Elk, of Harney Peak in the Dakotas, centers everywhere and nowhere, how afternoon thunderstorms blow in from the east, crash against sea cliffs, the Mayan coast, pile up, break, leave the Yucatan lowlands inches deep in flood—

*

Where there is water there is magic. Where there is magic there are always frogs, especially in the tropics, twenty species call like sharp, whistling voices of lost Mayan gods—The distended yellow eyes of the holy tree frog, royal digits, open mouths like burial urns—

*

Waist deep in natural history, the past spins like a great cycle that rolls back—different every time in content but not form, a calendar that spirals instead of flips, in four dimensional space, not flat and disconnected like old maps of the world, month to month, horizon to sharp horizon. There were monsters at the edges in 1492, but four hundred years later they are everywhere, and this season the same as the one called *Tuk* 830 years ago—

*

Trust the scripture of travel, of mystery and diversity, the frog night come back strong on animal voices of a thousand worldly gods. Live with contrast. Go south to learn. Make your way home, changed, through sloughs, past the shell blue Caribbean, pale pink temple condominiums, and praise the holy sun distended above the Gulf—

EROSION

Is geology a kind of poetry? Is orogeny, uplift, the syncopation
of named eons laid end-to-end? Were they really clanking toward

our future? Is geology the story we should put our hominid minds to?
Is the Anthropocene us, or are we all? Is geology poetry?

Is poetry geology? Does the numerate, have the upper hand,
or the numinous? Is that a shock of red cardinal flowers,

or is it hummingbird bustling between? Is it a buried sediment
to be assayed for carbon in the present, tested? Are carbon levels

to Geiger counter, as stock market is to CNBC? Is the latest species'
cha-cha toward oblivion our unrattled success?

Is this age the joke our sapiens ancestors wouldn't get?

THE GEOLOGIST SCRUTINIZES DINOSAURS IN THE ANTHROPOCENE

Pigeon genetic warriors strutting
through the Zagreb train station!
One impressive bobbing
global tribe. Pigeon nation take pride—
You have carried the heavy load
of your genes forward to reach the next eon.
You have arrived in your gray blazer
with ascot the color of shale, sorting
among the first crumbs of climate disruption—
Pink feet steady on the gritty pavement,
a small dot of pigment on your nose,
the jewelry of evolution, biological expression
adding a white dot on your skull's crown.
That nodding head, I could pick out
among a thousand competing avian species,
and yet you give me only a single comment—
A dab of green shit deposited after eye contact—
You—lowly, diminished neoaves—
I know where we will spend tonight
but not a night sixty-five million years from now—
Our rich niche secured by our own pecking.

EROSION

When a tree falls in the forest, forget that old
saw about whether it makes a sound if there's no

one there to hear it crash, ask instead how old it is,
and how long it will take to rot: they say a year's rot

for every one photosynthesizing, sunlight's energy
transforming water plus atmospheric carbon dioxide into

carbohydrates, (read, sugar) and builds rings of rich wood
breaking down over time, what we also call decomposition,

or its study, *taphonomy* from the Greek *taphos*, meaning "tomb"):
anyway, RIP A.R. Ammons, fallen father oak, rotting 12 years now,

unless, that is, you were cremated, or shot full of chemicals
and sunk like a common corpse in some mausoleum or crypt:

but sometimes fire doesn't do it, especially with poets, as they say,
the others, not the scientists, Percy Shelley's heart wouldn't

burn (says Lord Byron looking on) after he drowned in 1822:
I'm not telling you anything you don't know if you've read

The Oxford Book of Literary Anecdotes, a text slowly
rotting (literary leaves and branches) entombed in a book

made of wood pulp soon rotting itself on some shelf or in
some landfill (maintaining paper at 64 to 72 degrees

Fahrenheit is expensive, so rare): and what of poems as
opposed to anecdotes (from the Greek *anekdota*, "to publish"):

how are we to gauge a poem's afterlives and when, even,
are they dead? We know poems do not die with the poet

or the poet's family, no matter how hard they try to lock
them up in the tomb of the literary estate (a few dollars for

Frost, a fortune for T.S. Eliot), though sometimes
a stillborn poem never lives, like an oak spout burned

in the season's last frost, green and living for a moment,
but quickly mulch, a sip of nutrient for some recycler,

reduced to a swirl of slime in the duff's salad bar for
worms, flies, beetles, and aphids: and Archie, your poems

seeds planted and grown timber, still crisp as iceberg lettuce
as I read this summer from your *Garbage:* your heart did not

burn, but rots slowly in libraries all over, a forest of words:
but what if I burned *Garbage* on the beach, washed ashore

shipwrecked out of the great swirling Gulf Stream of poetry
the storm of publication, reviews, prizes, biographical

footnotes, annotations by critics: what would remain:
a rusting pile of semi-colons burnished by wind and rain,

like black BBs, salvaged punctuation, a pyramid of scrap metal
ball bearings, or the eyes of cartoon characters unlinked

rolling in the surf: Archie, I am with you as you drive
from Florida to Cornell and pass that smoking hulk

our tomb to the Unknown Poet for an Undeclared War:
Archie, the Forever Colossus of the Colon, filing

the colon's deed in the courthouse of poetry's signature
punctuations early on (Dickinson owns the dash, O'Hara

the exclamation point, Cummings the parenthesis
and bracket, a stock account of influence and subsidy)

your mark languishing centuries as merely a pointer
"okay, here comes a LIST:" — until you staked a claim

behind it: again, and again: and again: and again: "the quick
stop-and-go," the circle never closing, the rusty crank turning

two shelled peas planted, then harvested again, and again:
they who knew you claim you hated being pinned down

(how scientific, living synthesis) and you opened up the world's
tightening intellectual architecture, endless "what ifs." So, what if:

THE GEOLOGIST LAMENTS LIMESTONE

After Auden

If vacation, a formal suspension, can be carved
into the requisite strata of meaning, then *vacate* floats
like a continental pluton upon the molten mantle of our
lives—and we scramble for immediate footing amid the porous

Croatian limestone, the cliffs crumble offshore
as the near sea breaks often against our Beneteau's
fiberglass sides, a boat manufactured for cruising,
not the briny blue depths of living—a week healing here,

sage green ridges chafe around us, even underwater
the shadows of rock ribs appear in every sequential
harbor, the drowned country rock so soft it crumbles
in hand, or under foot climbing the Vis headlands,

but limestone offers some bracing frail foundation—
Mark these cliffs, then I will always remember—
Hear fully the rasping resident cyclic cicadas
onshore; examine my certainty of a life seen through

the blue windows of two earlier travertine waterfalls
and then the basin brimming with runoff at the bottom—
Just now, the white cottage high on the humming
hillside spotted through the rigging is maybe last night's

Zagreb summer couple who weekend on the island
and promenade on the quay with their Yorkie—
We would be foolish to discount the local cults housed
in cut stone temples the size of doghouses, weathered features

of ancient gods, hip-shot and fertile—they still greet this greedy
traveler and barter temporary treaties with the vanished
underworld half the planet from my own granite certainties—
Amid islands the sea built like a Betty Crocker layer cake,

each strata is past-baked, deposited shelf-by-shelf,
humps rounded by wind and water, hummocks of brush
buffeted by black, dead pines (beatle kills), a bathtub
drained and filled, drained and filled, a scum line

building up ages of dark crusty mineral shoreline
Phoenicians, Greeks, and Romans scoured for ports
and left their dead—we tack west over open water—
On the east flank of Bisevo is the Blue Cave, a grotto

weather-worn by eons of tides; we anchor there
and the boat swells and heaves. Security erodes until I cower—
The dinghy returns. My heart retreats, a tiny bilge pump of flesh
as the moment is flushed—the timid echo of kin, a whisper,

is only grotto-deep: "I am the tremor, the quaking
olive no one holds aloft. I am finally empty of lingering
affection for home. Love is no longer held in solution—
In this age we must split allegiances always between two places."

The brittle cliffs and the iPhone photographs do little
justice to the karst peeping through the porthole in the galley—
We motor on, the wind stays a stranger high in the ancient
walled groves, their mineral language scrawled over plunging.

FIELD NOTEBOOK: BURNING

Brush crackling underfoot cut months ago, piled for burning, dried by hot summer winds. Now flame staggers higher than my memory of any fire but two. Grasshoppers stirred from the Johnson grass by my patrol of the hot perimeter leap the wrong way and land in ash, soon roasted brittle grey. Their scissor legs by instinct hop from the following flame. The first fire over 60 years ago in Wisconsin, Aldo Leopold fighting a neighbor's trash fire spread to farmyard dry grass and weeds. Moving down hill toward planted pines. Aldo directing his wife and daughter, grabbing tools—a hose, buckets, a sprinkling can, broom, shovel—but the fire gained speed and Aldo instructed his wife to dip a gunny sack in marsh water and wet down any place that might catch spark. By that time there were a dozen neighbors fighting the fire. Flames were in the alders, and as Aldo crossed to wet down the grass before the advancing fire he collapsed, laid back, rested his head on a clump of unburned grass and crossed his hands on his chest. The fire swept lightly over his body and was gone.

Watching embers where life once filled the meadow, I remember childhood nightly television, 1968, and soldiers holding square metal Zippo lighters burning what they called "hooches" on patrol, and the flame climb the thatch like my racing friends on dark evenings in the suburbs before we were called home. Those old lighters, etched with skulls, Hueys, Geisha girls, block-lettered LOVE, or rice paddy wisdom: "We the unwilling trained by the unskilled to do the impossible for the ungrateful ten minutes too late." But mostly it's making art I see, you, Philip, setting up a portable easel and tracing the controlled burn's advancing or retreating line in a longleaf pine forest. Something lives in the fire that only your quick brush strokes can catch and save, ash and charcoal left on paper as the fire passes, art like the transforming act of burning, like Aldo's death, or the dream still lifting the vet's head, remembering the Zippo's finger of flame pointing at the eave and the old woman pleading, and the film crew backing away as the orange line crawls upward for the roof beam, the ragged pile collapsing into shattered motes of pure blue flame.

THE GEOLOGIST ON THE PLUTON

Old heat supports this poem composed
a thousand feet above the cove floor—
Natural history is a code I use to slough
a quarter billion years of erosion, the last
brief epoch supporting red oaks tattered
by wind and rain. Peregrines reef their
wings and plunge like weighted insults
in view of tourists trudged up from
the parking lot—dogs on leashes,
children dressed for Halloween
and one distraught father's sullen
directions to the derisive
summit. The view waivers as each
group files in to plug their value
into the waiting landscape's formula—
Someone points out a quarry so distant
the worked rock looks like a nick
in wedding china at a yard sale—
Another spots the pond like an eye
never blinking, pinched open by fringes
of forest brindled by November shadow—
Three women ask for their picture snapped
with corrugated ridges framing their pose—
They could be on the Empire State Building
if not for the overlook set on pure gneiss
and no elevator save for my imagination.

EROSION

"Won't almost any theory bear revision?
To err is human, not to, animal."
    — Robert Frost, "The White-Tailed Hornet"

maybe the Anthropocene demanded the colon: the chemistry of rot
equal parts building up and tearing down, a balanced equation

the seesaw of wedded actions, a barbell with round balls
on either extreme, win/lose, time split between the dugout and

hard against the warning path: like on Monday how I saw a
compost pit at a local college, a mound ten feet high, 4/5s

wood chips, grass trimmings, yard debris, and 1/5 cafeteria
food waste (corncobs, steak trimmings, wilted salad, napkins,

fried potatoes, soggy pizza crust) turned by a front-end loader
once a week, and when broken open with a pitchfork, a million black

soldier fly larvae worked inside, like a business district of decay,
a street party of pulsing worms eating what we think of as trash,

garbage, debris to be disappeared in landfills: the light is all
this world needs to thrive and be welcomed back into the living:

the small segmented maggots of the black soldier fly
a community, a growth industry, a segment of our economy

over-performing with unemployment at zero (birthed into labor
and grown strong on heavy lifting), and yet around us,

the leaves hauled away or burned, and the kitchen scraps
end up in the garbage or septic tank or ground, and diluted

and flushed through sewers, and we pay not to see black
bags full of droppings, shed skin, husks, tailings, trimmings,

cans, plastic bags, used baby diapers, hair, toenail clippings,
boxes, sheathings, caps, tampons, broken utensils, extra pills

(these more often flushed down toilets with ticks and condoms)
straws, Styrofoam cups (average useful life expectancy 15 minutes):

so, that list out of the way, let's get back to the end of the barbell,
the living, active end, the "I-got-up-this-morning-and-all-my-vital-signs

strong,-so-I'll-get-out-of-bed-and-try-to-write-some-poetry" end of
the human spectrum, and is this really that different than a single

black soldier fly larva about its work? Is making poetry out of observed
experience really that far afield from bacteria dissolving shit in

a composting toilet, or maggots chewing up a corn cob in a pile of
wood chips (the iambic throb of cicadas in the background trees not

lost on anyone who pays attention to such cycles): that poetry is
compost is not an original idea, and if I were an academic I might

even have a footnote here (thank you Walt Whitman) to set
any reading mind in motion backward, which is not that unusual

a move since I've already brought Shelley and Byron into this
field of inquiry, and they've been dead and rotted for 200 years

(that is, except for Shelley's heart— remember?—which Mary
Shelley wrapped in one of Shelley's poems and stored in a drawer

for 30 years before the shriveled organ, one of our greatest hearts
in the language, was finally buried in Dorsett, England 1850): there

is no telling where this inquiry will end, and make fertile soil, as it
could soldier on (like the fly) for pages more, or abruptly cease in

mid-sentence (Shelley's heart burning) like an abandoned mine
shaft sent down into someone's claim that missed the mother lode:

FIRST LIFE, ROTTING LIFE

hunters dumped two deer
in slack water behind the shoals
one whole decapitated buck
and a small doe butchered

her head trailing
like a flesh buoy
the stripped spine and shanks
gnawed by hungry bass

a lens into a community
of strangers, their action
completed cycles
the deer stalked then shot

committed back
to river water and silence

EROSION

I have poured myself into this borrowed vessel,
then stepped back to see me overflow; I have watched a liquid

leave the eyes of two dying dogs, and slip, a golden stream
over the sides, and pool below:

CIRQUE OF THE TOWERS

> glacial country
> ten thousand seasons
> snow-shaped, these ridges

Wolf's Head, Pingora, Mitchell Peak, spires and jagged rock. Lodge pole pines skirmish with glacial till for a hold. Moraines like waves on the cirque's slow geologic tide. Texas Pass in the distance, still snow there, and beyond, more wild country. The rest of the world recedes down the trail at my back, men and women in cars somewhere beyond our 12-mile hike in over Big Sandy Pass. Eight days here.

> rock wall gray-shadowed
> with first cirque sun
> rustle of pine needles

> someone calling
> another down near
> Lonesome Lake

The sun finally over Mitchell Peak. Warm sweet warm sun. So cold this morning, maybe now the gloves can come off. Wind yesterday. Bent two tent poles. Front right and rear right. Wind out of the north, sprinting across the cirque.

> boulders pines wind
> another high country poem
> like Rexroth's
> out there waiting somewhere

Tomorrow we return—no more mosquitoes, dirty socks, back to all the crust we call civilization. My heart is larger here, pumps a little truer, as if I remember a past when the world was like this—not just the altitude, or the glacier's slow work, or the pines fighting the cold for their share. Not like that. Something more. Some idea of space and us.

             like harmony
        call it time to sit and see
    hear a rock slide on a distant cirque wall

A sparrow wobbles through the grass, fat on gorp. The sun
stumbles past the high continental divide. When I cross it
I'll spit, splitting the difference, forget my face, bearded
here, when I shave it off.

           pines won't care I've left
                 no return
             no leaving either

FIELD NOTEBOOK: ANTELOPE AMONG CATTLE

As landscape, antelope are the tan wind. Cows are stones in the field. On a crumbling bluff hillside outside of Sheridan for a moment they look like cows among cows. It's that fences don't stop them. They leap into the imagination in an atavistic way—as a snake on the road is never mistaken for a stick. A little bit of Pleistocene in Wyoming, their faces thick with the weight of a species worth of horns and rut. Cars pass and antelope mediate the distance.

Then antelope are a breeze from the 19th century. Two antelope watch the Wagon Box Fight, just below a line of pines, Fort Phil Kearny stark beyond the horizon. Red Cloud circled the wagons on a spotted pony. It was a true western, soldiers out to cut wood, pulling the flat wagons in a long line, and Red Cloud brooding in a draw, already a mountain. He shook his lance and circled as warriors circled like prairie hawks. The antelope were already the wind, or maybe they were winter coming on. The antelope were not annoyed by the first Springfield repeating rifles. This was a sign, the Sioux and Cheyenne falling like cottonwood leaves, Red Cloud and the battle moving like prairie fire through sage, the gunpowder smells.

Antelope keep their distance today, grazing still among cattle just off the interstate. Antelope carry their pronghorns among the cattle as Red Cloud carried his lance among the soldiers. The cows carry their immense resignation up and down the pastures as wild antelope watch, mysterious as Red Cloud.

Men and antelope are strange to each other. Separate kingdoms. "Will you ever know what I am thinking," I whisper in the direction of the distant antelope, not exactly to them. "Just listen, just listen."

THE GEOLOGIST SPEAKS OF PHOSPHATE

They were lucky to mine what once was only ooze,
a mineral that looks like (is) fish roe, a gold strike
for the men who found it, who owned it, by hook or crook

or quit claim deed, now history, photos on a website,
a footnote in a geology book. But without that ooze
we would not exist. By us I mean me, you,

New Carolinians, the whole of the New South.
In that ooze began one of many new beginnings—
Not an oil strike like Texas, but phosphate, just as rich,

but a short-lived commodity—ancient fish shit
in veins 6 to 36 inches thick, settled in shallows
by oligocene, miocene, and pliocene tides and currents,

a geologic jackpot spread like mayonnaise below,
the buried economic beginning after the end,
at least for farming, as post-war entrepreneurial

clodhoppers donned their slouch hats, abandoned
40 acres and a mule, dropped their hoes, strode out
of cotton fields and found in rich mineral seams

an extravagance of profit, a future—from farmer
to middleman to boss man investor in cotton mills
and railroads, shiny-suited merchants selling wagonloads

of fertilizer to neighbors for cotton acres of gullied
upcountry, slick-talking know-it-alls on muleback
in midstate sandy ridge fields selling porch-to-

porch their miracle of agricultural productivity,
maybe not a revolution in human purpose, but for
sure in wealth, geology intersecting with sociology

right here, one strike in a straight line
of South Carolina boom and bust economies
playing out geologist James Hutton's "we find no

vestige of a beginning,–no prospect of an end,"
not to the earth's record in rock but to somebody's
get rich quick fixes for a deadly poor state,

poorly run (with squandered human resources).
In that sense BMW is no different than our rice,
gold, canals, cotton, textiles, or phosphate.

Only in duration do they differ. I see farmers
slathering rows with shovel loads of deep time's
rich fruit and byproduct, buried millions of years,

and yes, springing forth fertility to pad bank
accounts, even pull a few upward from Hard Luck
to Easy Street, but also perpetrate the Powerball

dreams of the South Carolina poor, to catapult
hopes from Here (pork-n-beans and Spam) to There
(T-Bone) in one long stride, to strike it rich, move on.

TEXT BOOK

An elucidated landscape,
a lecture of color and hue
like strata both natural
and cultural—Washington
Irving's imagination
burrowed deep into existing
Dutch sources, and then
painters like Church
create uplifts
of big river, mountains,
sky, a school where views

transport visions
upward to fall like small
streams over sharp
precipices to shatter
below and flow—
Riches followed
and turreted mansions
of cut limestone quarried
paid for by canvases
pooled in museums
and parlors downstream.

From the second floor
of the guest house—
A cut lawn and hydrangeas
past their prime,
a line of maples
layered in darkness
at 6:30, and a crow
answering another
in the distance,
a language not
unlike Dutch or English—

Some robber baron
erected Mayan ruins
along the Hudson's shore
to teach those passing
in steamboats
the world does not end
but spreads, from many
sources like ripples.

On the lawn above
the river three
college boys climb
the intricate branches
of an elm to the very
top and I had to look
away, for fear they
would fall, yet youth
clings to high places
just as old age huddles
below and looks up.

Somewhere nearby
Rip Van Winkle slept
and woke to changes
in the glacial valley,
still here
and yes to come
to all those who sleep.

I am awake
for this moment,
a cool late September,
wind animating one tree
with the sky behind
just turned sodalite's
subtle blue.

POEM WITHOUT AN END

The crow Gowri found
yesterday dying at
the end of the island,
and 24 rescued snapping
turtle eggs, and how

she hatched out 23—
She has a skill with
suffering I say, like tracing
faults in fins of rock,
cleavages where seams

break open. By this
I don't mean Gowri
is sad, but she absorbs
suffering as rocks
do rain, each drop

an acid, eroding
over deep time—
Like how Liz shows
Catherine lichen dying
from the center outward

And I remember
Catherine's painting
of the red wing
blackbird coming
apart at the seams—

The crow is somewhere,
maybe retreated
to crevice or overhang,
say it, to heal or die—
We hear other crows

and church bells
across the river—
For now, the shale
looks stable
in the morning light.

EROSION

the Dixie Hummingbirds in town to sing one final time before
Ira Tucker died, and driving around Spartanburg Ira's story

of this Southern town in the 1930s: a cantaloupe plant
growing downtown and Ira watering it every day for a month

and the vine growing, like Jack and the beanstalk, long and huge
winding around the vacant Main Street lot, green leaves like a

fleur-de-lis thriving, spreading, taking light in and the green vine
along, and Ira's one cantaloupe increasing in size and ripening

until he finally comes to pick it and it was gone, just like that
and though Ira did not say stolen, that's what I inferred

from the story: somehow I was implicated, though I was born
twenty years later, but being guilty I was determined not

to steal Ira's cantaloupe again, and so we worked hard
to put on a good show, though from the west came a huge

thunderstorm and washed out the last few numbers, including
the long-anticipated "Love Me Like a Rock":

this morning a ruby-throated hummingbird flew
from cardinal flower to coreopsis, and there was the screech owl's

single note in these particular woods, and the sun, late today
showed no sign it would disappoint the high expectations

of morning, and though earth's clocks are always trustworthy
and a squirrel had succeeded in his endless backyard plot to clear

the feeder, and morning's arrival had prolonged a few minutes
into light, and several aqua-tailed lizards were awake along the wall

and dark rocks line the flower bed, little grottoes holding the short lives
of the cold-blooded and naturally blue: I still hoped for a long life

among the caterpillars, broad-headed skinks, and the cardinal
with the red feathers vanished from his red head, and all

this was only a seedbed of instances, each species a species of intent:
and yes, I falter here, remember two days ago a red-shouldered hawk

fly-ridden in the center lane and how it vanished overnight
the road cleared by fox or coyote, carted off to feed the pups:

this day, yes even this poem ends (you guessed it) with
a storm and rain, more inches piling up, almost ten

a month, the yard a misplaced rainforest, and lightning
thunder moving through: now that we have Doppler (on both

devices— iPhone, iPad) we've started to worry more about
the trees, but sadly not in an ecological sense: instead

in a deductible sense: waterlogged lawns and houses
all over town this summer with trees fallen through

roofs, far beyond remembered lumber, and cracked rafters
2X6s long before the latest flora holocaust (hemlock, willow

oak, red bay): worry, yes, we pray the homeowner's prayer:
there's no silver lining in low premiums and the shit hits

the fan for everyone in their time, so give up, unless
you take a photo and through Photoshop paint a lining here

after the fact: back to the garden gauge, filled up three times
already this month, a silver lining for slugs and mosquitoes

and me if we ever veer back to drier seasons, but when would
that be? The Pleistocene's long gone, and if this place

ever looked dry as the Olduvai Gorge there's no sign of it now:
but seriously, this thing has to end, as all storms must:

bang/whimper/fizzle stick, or the last ball in the side pocket
the storm's on its last leg and our big oak still stands

sucker now for some future tree disease: Doppler shows Charlotte's
under a red watch, the Queen City, our neighbors to the east

I wouldn't turn my back on that tree though, since sometimes
we hear one fall in the deep woods long after the wind

pushes through—Ira's it's a damn shame there is no law
especially gravity, can save us from our own surprises:

FAWN IN A HAY BALE

The black snake in the median
twisted into an unanswered
question is to the bloody
point. No swerving. No faltering
as any machine rolls fecklessly forward—
Then to open a hay bale
and find the paired ebony hooves
still shiny, the auburn hair
and splintered bones hidden
no more in the side-long silo—

Death is a combine—
Death is a spring morning
smelling of straw and diesel.

THE GEOLOGIST SURVEYS KEY SWAMP TRAIL

Feathers among fallen
green walnuts, a hawk or larger
constellation of fox or feral cat?
Maypops nearby offer globed
sweetness, but not rich package
of protein of compact songbird
nabbed in furtive flight moment
or one lousy screw-up stall
that led to bounty for another

Like the tobacco crop
rolled to market in 500 pound
barrels, centuries of cash
for prosperous countryside,
but stripping the soil,
enslaving the workers,
an economy still recent
and way less sustainable
compared to this trailside
kill site of hawk or cat

On cut-over edges cottontails
thrive and scamper when
I pass, their fur too often
a token of food chains
functioning. Here what
we now call "natural capital"
stored in fallow fields—
Soybeans, bird bodies,
locust sprouted and decayed—
Return is hunt and farm fields,
also tourist trade from far off

This morning I feed on it all—
Take notes, draw pictures,
outline brief captured histories
among stratified layers of culture—

Human and natural history
stacked, crosshatched—
Feathers fallen on a trail

ONE TROUBLE

Remembering Peter Mattheissen
(1927-2014)

Twenty years ago I camped
at Watson Place with students,
a rare, dry land Wilderness
Waterway site, north of Key Largo
with Watson's own cistern
and its long-broken sides;
we'd canoed in from Everglades City
and the students had read
Killing Mr. Watson, and so literature
crossed with adventure in
what passed back then for
rare eastern back country—
One of those students is dead
a suicide years later
and I still tell the story of how
on that, his first canoe trip,
we pointed him off solo into
the marsh, and emerging
he'd said, "A week ago I didn't know
what a mangrove is, and now I'm
shitting in 'em."

                    *

An above-ground cistern
rectangular walls, the ash-gray
weathered concrete carbonated
in hot, beat-down Florida sun—
standing off Carol Sand Road
on North Key Largo, the sides so
high you can climb up to see—
Ash-bins of history have nothing
on abandoned human infrastructure,
lost lesson loitering in the brush,
old sugar place maybe,

sweat-stained Panama brims
the only shade, black bodies
leading a mule around a creaking
cane press, long dust.

*

And up north, Edgar Watson,
but not really Watson—
just a novelist's version
of Watson, headed deep
into the 10,000 Islands,
the first motorboat anybody's
heard in the sawgrass and
mangrove flats. "Only trouble's
interesting," say the fiction
workshops; that's how to write
a story, and two generations
stinking with trouble, this maybe
the last, or one of the last, to think
that's the way out, the crux.

*

Then there was the green
water, dark, absorbing
Florida heat, generating
an internal circulation,
flowing in one direction
along the long, punky
concrete sides, and then
reversing in opposition
to meet in the soupy middle.

*

A decade earlier I was
a college student and camped
at Shark River Chickee
on my first Wilderness Waterway
trip, and when I thought I was

in deep, a cigarette boat
pulled up and a woman
got off to pee in the park service
chemical toilet and came out
with her pants around
her knees, screaming
snake! snake! And her boyfriend,
a Miami policeman we soon
found out, jumped off the boat's
bow with a magnum pistol
to blow away the coiled eastern
diamondback rattling in the privy.

        *

One trouble
and one solution, no box
lid shut, crafted
cleanly by inwardness;
what we don't know,
subliminal rituals
of chance and surprise,
awareness of our
capacity to forget
as well as remember,
reminders of where we
linger, and the going on
from there; now, the coming
of all into one fate,
the only fate, the fact
that is our animal conclusion.

        *

The green water
I thought of as
algae, though now

I'm sure it was
cyanobacteria—

I couldn't see
an inch below
the surface.

*

In the cistern dead raccoons
turned in the water, five or six
on the surface, some fully furred,
others with little hair
so their skin showed yellow
as the animals bloated, and finally
sank. Coming for fresh water,
rare in the Keys, they'd fallen
in, the surface down two feet
so they couldn't climb out—
The floaters were recent
and as each rotted
their carcass disappeared.

*

This poem salvages
the rattlesnake through story,
though their populations
dwindle over most of their range—
and anecdote brings back
my dead student, but that's
no solace for living or dead
as the rattler's bones dissolved
in marsh mud too
and I haven't thought of my
student in years, and now
the 'glades have filled
with pythons from Asia
and everyone's trying to shoot
them like fish in a barrel—
there's even a contest
to control the invasives

backed up by biologists.

*

A door out of the dark,
not a door in—

*

The last photo I saw
of Peter Mattheissen he
was nothing but bone
and angles, weathered
by eighty-six years—
I did not know him
except through novels
and the nonfiction he compared
to making cabinets,
all craft and no magic—
What would he make
of Auden's remembrance
of Yeats, and how
the dead man's
words survive, "modified
in the guts of the living?"
If he was great we will
only know by his books,
how well they resist
the circling currents
and the nervous reading
habits of the young.

*

Was it the young raccoons
fallen in, or the old masters
of the island dipping down
for one more privileged drink?

*

Starting with that image,
retrieved from the past,
how the sun shown on the green
water of that scummy cistern
and the troupe of gyrating raccoons,
beautiful if you look at it just right,
but what I'm ending with is
the bones, the settled bones
always at the bottom of things
dissolving, a chalky paste,
a felled forest of endings and lesser
beginnings as scapula, femur,
tibia, radius, ulna, vertebra,
break down, and even hubris merges
into a final calcite layer where all
if not one is close to one,
looking down through a window,
and someday it opens for me.

NETTLE

"... the yellow roots of nettles creep onward in the soil ..."
    —W. G. Sebald

Some say plants can stand in for personalities,
a sort of zodiac of field, garden, woods, as in
pining away, or feeling ginger, or even cherry—

Most are benign but dark-leaved, can't be mistaken
for bucolic, stinging with the voracity of vegetable
jelly-fish. I knew, but leaned anyway for a better
look through a tumble-down window—

Chairs with missing legs, bed frames, stacks of burlap
feed bags—and the nettle close by the mossy sill
pocked my sunny mood with prickled heat.

RATHLIN ISLAND

Not the sweet stink rising
from Bull Point's puffins, or the kittiwake
colony, or the blue eye just winked
open on the wind-lashed lough,
or the verge of prickly purple heather,
but the peregrine's sickle-hinged
stoop over fields above Cooraghy Bay—
a blade sharp as any grizzly tooth
pierced the air and dropped
below the basalt cliff face—
Strop every ribbon of surprise
to keep it sharp—

THE GEOLOGIST CONSIDERS THE POST-PASTORAL

The sewer piper clogged with sand—
Underwear abandoned at the old swimming
hole. Privet across the creek chokes

out dog-hobble and mountain laurel,
an infestation, though once preferred by settlers,
a topiary possibility topping off the lush

natives. In this unsettled critical turn
we see there is no room for the old order,
flexibility is paramount, the epoch's defense—

Only the seismic shift, coarse volcano dust,
meteor strike cants the conversation earthward—
We are now the voice, the digital gramophone

much more than the owl in the neighbor's
wood lot. His song is stilled by the mirror
of the world, though he doesn't know or care

like we do with our archives of unwasted signs,
the lyrics and poems of unintended martyrs
to modernity, troubadours of academic detachment—

I want to open a door where we could walk
into something like now. It's simple physics—
There is no past unless we make it with paper,

or better yet, keys beneath our elongated fingers—
The past is a funhouse mirror and the future is black magic.

NOTES

The coming and/or already arrived age can either be pronounced "anTHrəpə sēn" or as I prefer, "anTROP asēn."

The first epigraph is from *Kosmokolos Global Climate Tragi-Comedy* (2011) by Bruno Latour Frederique Ait-Touati & Chloe Latour.

The collection's second epigraph from, Hank Williams, is from an important poem composed either near the end of the Holocene, or the beginning of the Anthropocene, depending on your perspective.

"Voice, While it Lasts" was written several years before I read Charles Siebert's "Of a Feather" (*New York Times Magazine*, 1.31.16) and his heartbreaking paragraph about highly social species: "It is one of those unlikely natural outcomes of the so-called anthropocene, the first epoch to be named after us: the prolonged confinement of intelligent and social creatures, compelling them to speak the language of their keepers."

"The Geologist Knows God Plays Dice" is for Don McKay.

"DOR" is shorthand for how field biologists designate animals killed on highways. Road kill is a unique development of the Anthropocene.

"Fish with Head Still On" is for Nikky Finney.

"Field Notes: Spring" is after Robert Hass and is a homage to his rhythms and genius attention to place.

"The Geologist Anticipates the End of the Long Count" refers to the ancient Mayan system of keeping track of vast tracks of time. Archeologists agree the Long Count began on August 11, 3114 BC and many calculated that The Great Cycle (a portion of the Long Count) would end on December 21, 2012. This system stands in interesting contrast to geologic time as figured by geologists. As Scottish geologist James Hutton famously put it in the mid-nineteenth century, "no *vestige* of a beginning, no *prospect* of an end." And thanks to Ab Abercombie for taking me on his crocodile expeditions to Mexico in the late 1970s and early 1980s. The gift still endures with no prospect of an end.

"The Truth About the Present" is after Bei Dao.

"After the Great Acceleration" refers to the antropocene theory that the second half of the 20th century is unique in the history of human life, and possibly life itself. The early adopters of this theory have pointed to ice core records, climate change, species extinction rates and other indications of remarkable impact of our species on the natural environment.

"The Geologist Laments Limestone" borrows a few of tropes from Auden's monumental "In Praise of Limestone," and several other great limestone poems.

"Field Notebook: Burning" is for Philip Juras. The description of Aldo Leopold's death fighting a neighbor's fire was adapted from *Aldo Leopold His Life and Work* by Curt Meine (Madison: University of Wisconsin Press, 1988). Leopold could be seen as one of the last great philosophers of the holocene or one of the first in the Anthropocene.

"First Line, Rotting Life" is after George Oppen.

"The Geologist Surveys Key Swamp Trail" takes as its starting point Old St. Mary's City in Maryland. Many thanks to Kate Chandler for inviting me up to teach, read, and explore.

The initial draft of "One Trouble" was written during the 2014 Conference on the Sowell Collection for Literature, Community, and the Natural World at Texas Tech University in Lubbock, Texas. Many thanks to Barry Lopez for his reflective comments on Mattheissen's death that closed the conference, and to Kurt Caswell and Jim Warren for commenting on early versions. Thanks to Thomas Rain Crowe for suggesting the title.

"The Geologist Considers the Post-Pastoral" is for Terry Gifford, the ultimate post-pastoral poet.

As for the whole manuscript and a few individual poems and for giving me words to think with about the Anthropocene, thanks to the late John Harrington, Kaye Savage, Terry Ferguson, Brent Martin, Drew Lanham, and Catherine Reid. Thanks also to Nikky Finney, Ray McManus, Patrick Whitfill, and G.C. Waldrep for reading and commenting in various early, middle, and late stages of this production.

And for always, thank you Betsy Teter, love of my life.